Animals
of Land, Sea, and Air

By
Stéphanie Babin

Illustrated by
Marion Billet
Hélène Convert
Julie Mercier
Emmanuel Ristord

Twirl

Contents

Observing Animals 58

More to Know

Index 90

 The "Let's Review!" pages at the end of each section help reinforce learning.

 The "More to Know" section at the end of the book provides additional information to help you understand the subject.

Index Quickly find the word you're looking for with the index at the end of the book.

Look for the colored boxes in the bottom right-hand corners. You will find references to related subjects in other parts of the book.

What Is an Animal?

 Animals

An animal is a living being that eats, sleeps, moves, uses its senses, and needs food, water, and shelter to survive.

gives birth

lion

dies

Thomson's gazelle

swims

platypus

flies

pelican

slithers

cobra

walks

alpaca

eats

cow

chimpanzee   **chameleon**

Some care for their young.

Surinam toad   **spotted deer**

What
makes you an animal

?

You are a living being. You eat, sleep, move, and use your senses. So you *are* an animal! However, humans are able to do things that other animals can't.

We walk upright, and we have a brain that allows us to create and reason.

People share this planet with all animals and plants. It's important that we work together to make sure there are enough resources for everyone.

Threatened or Endangered **84**
Extinct Animals **86**

Animal Bodies

There are millions of species of animals in the world. No matter where they live—on a farm, in the ocean, or in the mountains—animals' bodies have adapted to their environment.

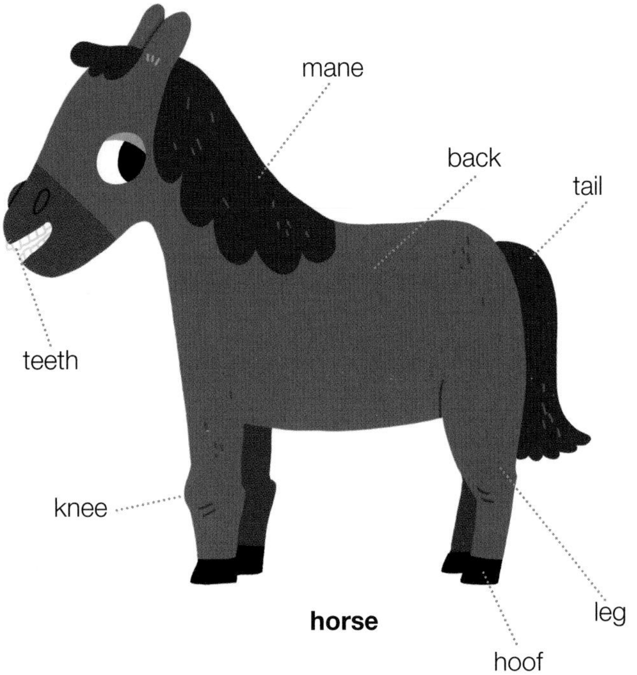

horns

mane

back

tail

fur

teeth

knee

belly

leg

udder

horse

hoof

cow

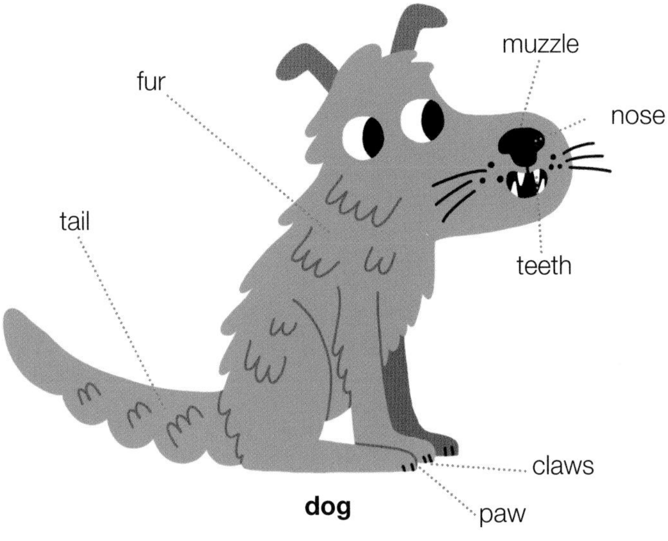

beak

fur

muzzle

nose

tail

teeth

feathers

wing

claws

claws

dog

paw

bald eagle

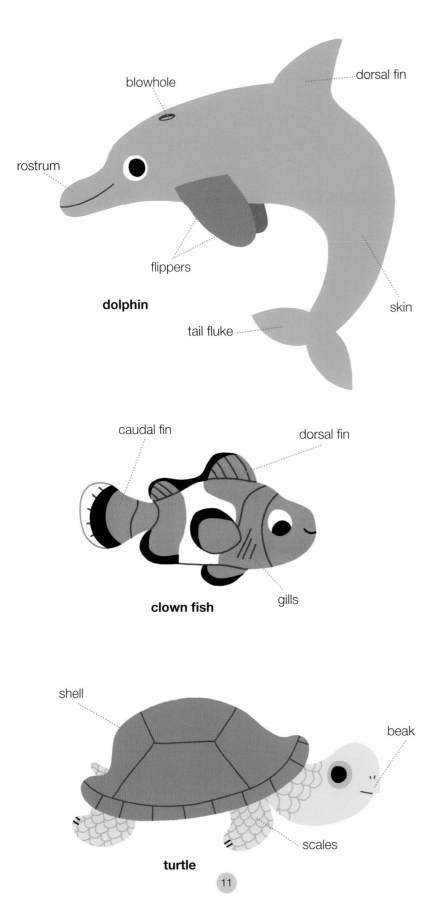

blowhole

dorsal fin

rostrum

flippers

dolphin

skin

tail fluke

caudal fin

dorsal fin

clown fish

gills

shell

beak

turtle

scales

11

All animals have some body parts that help them protect themselves or find food. Cats have whiskers, which they use to feel around them.

Geckos have thousands of tiny hairs on each foot, and each hair has hundreds of bristles. The hairs and bristles work together to help them grip surfaces.

Hedgehogs are prickly creatures, with about 5,000 spines on their back. When they feel threatened, they protect themselves by raising their spines. Be careful!

Types of Animals **14**
Footprints **88**

 # Diet

Depending on their diet, or what they eat, animals can be carnivores, herbivores, or omnivores.

vulture

lion

gazelle

Carnivores eat meat, the flesh of other animals.

seal

Herbivores eat plants.

cow

giraffe

parrotfish

sea turtle

orangutan

Omnivores eat both meat and plants.

gull

mouse

You might have been scared when you saw a lion capturing a gazelle on TV, and thought that the lion was really mean.

The lion was only doing what is natural behavior in the animal world. Animals hunt to feed themselves and their young.

Lions are carnivores, so they eat meat. What do you like to eat?

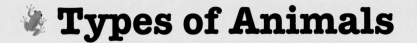

Types of Animals

Mammals are warm-blooded and have hair or fur, and the babies drink their mother's milk.

whale

aye-aye

common marmoset

skunk

zebu

narwhal

dog

tapir

manatee

porcupine

Amphibians are cold-blooded creatures that don't have hair.

salamander

tree frog

toad

Fish live only in water, have fins, and breathe using gills.

sturgeon

flying fish

monkfish

sailfish

sole

goldfish

eel

whale shark

seahorse

Reptiles breathe with their lungs.
Their thick skin is covered in scales.

Birds have feathers and wings.
They lay eggs with hard shells.

caiman

lizard

flying
dragon

leatherback sea turtle

iguana

rattlesnake

coral snake

hummingbird

swan

auk

kingfisher

heron

falcon

Invertebrates don't have a spine, but they may have a hard shell, or an "outside skeleton" called an exoskeleton.

earthworm

jellyfish

fly

butterfly

coral

tarantula

locust

mussel

crab

sea cucumber

snail

 # Mammals

Most mammals give birth to live young. The babies drink their mother's milk after they are born.

This female **cat** is pregnant.

After she gives birth to a litter of kittens,

she feeds them her milk

and takes care of them.

Baby **giraffes** fall about 6 feet (2 meters) to the ground when they are born.

.... pouch

Baby **kangaroos**, called **joeys**, stay in their mother's pouch until they are around seven to 10 months old.

Baby **dolphins** are born tail-first and can swim on their own right after birth.

How
many babies do animals have at a time ?

Humans usually give birth to one baby at a time. Some mammals are the same way, but many can give birth to several babies at once.

A litter is a group of babies born at the same time. Dogs have about five or six puppies in a litter. Other mammals that have litters are cats, mice, and pigs.

It's not common for humans to have more than one baby at a time, but it happens! Two babies born at the same time are called twins.

Animals That Lay Eggs

Oviparous animals lay eggs that develop outside the mother's body. These animals include birds, reptiles, insects, and fish.

chicken

egg

A **hen** lays eggs,

nest

keeps them warm,

chick

eggshell

watches the chicks hatch,

and shows them how to eat.

Sea turtles lay their eggs in the sand.

lizard

snail

fish

ostrich

An **emperor penguin** keeps its egg safe and warm on top of its feet.

Where
is the chick
in the egg
you eat

?

Eggs are nutritious, and you might love to eat them! Hens lay eggs with or without roosters, but a rooster is necessary for a chick to grow inside an egg.

Farms that raise chickens for edible eggs make sure that no roosters are around. This means that the eggs you eat won't have chicks in them!

Eggs can be fried, scrambled, boiled, made into an omelet, and used to make pastries and cakes. What's your favorite way to eat eggs?

Types of Animals 14

Caring for Their Young

Some baby animals are able to survive on their own soon after birth. Other animals are cared for by their parents for a while. These parents have many tasks!

chickadees

feeding

emperor penguins

keeping warm

lion

protecting **wild boar**

bears

disciplining

cleaning

deer

spiders

carrying

orangutans

teaching

dolphins

koalas

guiding

wolves

hunting

You have adults who take care of you, and you need them. It doesn't always happen that way with animals.

Koalas take care of their young. Other animals, such as sea turtles or lizards, live on their own as soon as they're born.

A rabbit can have many babies in a year. Rabbits feed their young until the bunnies leave the nest when they're two to three weeks old.

Metamorphosis

Some creatures transform completely as they develop from an egg to an adult.

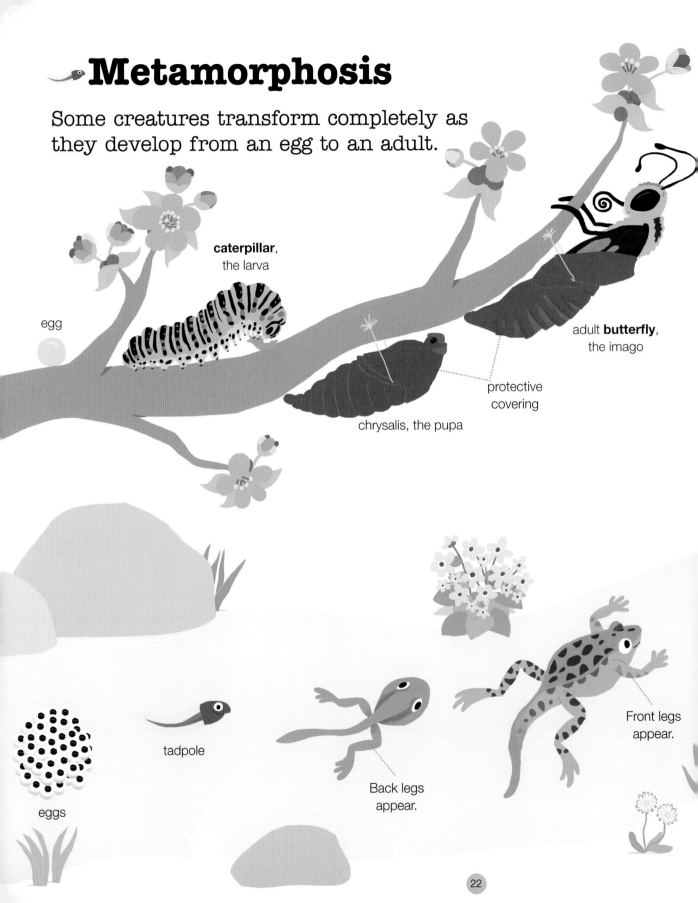

caterpillar, the larva

egg

chrysalis, the pupa

protective covering

adult **butterfly**, the imago

eggs

tadpole

Back legs appear.

Front legs appear.

When the butterfly's wings are dry, it flies away!

adult **frog**

Your body gradually changes throughout your lifetime. You don't change your appearance the way a butterfly or frog does.

Children grow a little at a time until they become adults. They put on weight, grow taller, and develop muscles. Their lungs, heart, and brain grow too!

Once you're an adult, you don't grow taller, but you can gain weight and lose muscle. It's important for people and animals to stay fit and healthy.

Let's Review!

How do these animals move?

Who eats what? Match the plates of food to the correct person or creature.
Are they a carnivore, herbivore, or omnivore?

Which animals belong to the same group? What's similar about them?

Can you match the baby animals to their parents?

All animals change as they grow.
What stages do they go through?
How have you changed as you have grown?

Animal Life

 # Shelter

Many animals have a place where they can eat, sleep, hide, or meet other animals like them.

bees in a natural hive

beehive box

chickadees in their nest

sole on the sandy seafloor

hermit crab in its shell

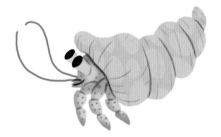

flea in a dog's fur

bats in their cave

clown fish in a sea anemone

mole in its tunnel

deer in a bush

spider in its web

Where
are animals' homes
?

Some animals, such as sharks and caribou, don't really have a home. They wander in search of food. Bees, however, return to their hives several times a day.

Many birds migrate, following a set route at the same time every year. They travel hundreds of miles from colder regions to warmer ones.

Other animals, including hedgehogs, hibernate. After storing up food in the fall, they sleep in their homes all winter long and wake again in the spring.

beaver in its lodge

mussels on a rock

bear at its den

ants in their anthill

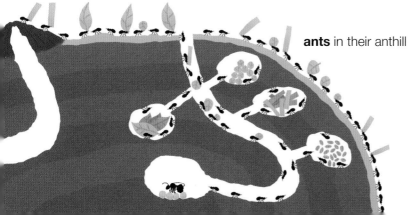

 # Sleep

All animals sleep, some at night, others during the day—but each of them has their own way of getting some shut-eye.

bat

upside down

dog

paws in the air

sloth

hangs onto a branch

lion cubs

snuggle close to their mother

horse

stands up

chimpanzee

holds on to its mother's back

red-eared sliders

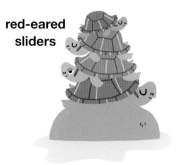

high and dry on a rock

walrus

on a rock in the sun

flamingo

stands on one leg

parrot

tucks its head under its wing

pangolin

curls up in a ball

shark

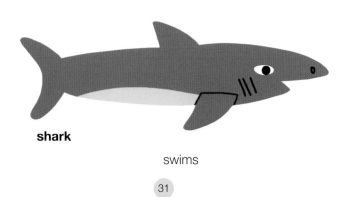

swims

When
do animals sleep

?

You sleep at night, and you might take a nap in the afternoon. Some animals do the same thing, but others don't! Every species has its own sleep cycle.

Many animals, including owls, are nocturnal. That means they are active at night. They might hunt for food, eat, or drink then.

Some animals hibernate to conserve energy when the weather gets cold. Those include bears, groundhogs, and some reptiles, insects, and amphibians.

Shelter **28**
Night Forest **52**

Communication

Animals can communicate in different ways: with their voices or special body features, or by their expressions, behaviors, and postures.

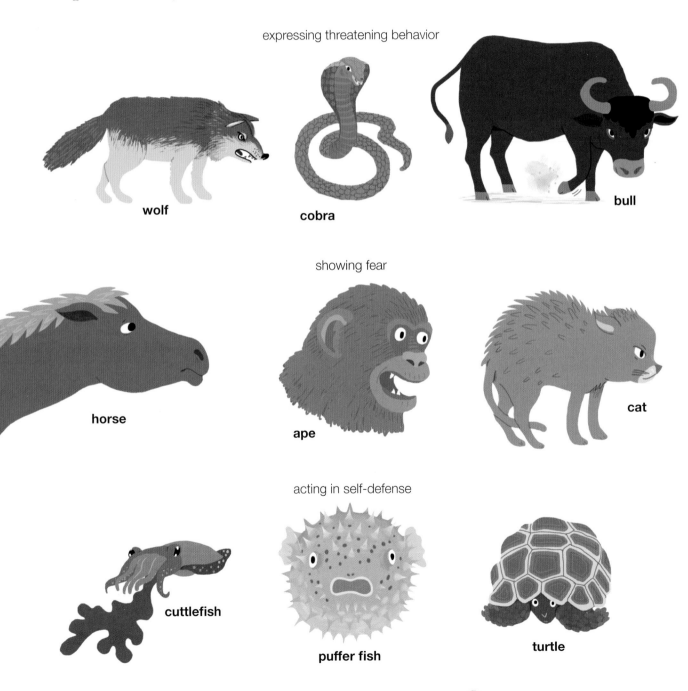

expressing threatening behavior

wolf

cobra

bull

showing fear

horse

ape

cat

acting in self-defense

cuttlefish

puffer fish

turtle

playing

dolphin **seal**

marking their territory

dog **wild boar**

showing joy

dog **ape**

attracting a mate

peacock **deer**

Birds' songs can be beautiful, but they are actually not singing because they are musical. They just want to talk to each other!

The songs can mean that the birds are in their own territory. The males might also sing to attract females.

Singing is a useful way for birds to recognize others in their flock too. Have you noticed the differences in the songs of various birds?

Sounds Animals Make

A dog barks.

A cat meows.

A cat purrs.

A cow moos.

A sheep bleats.

A pig grunts.

A turkey gobbles.

A chicken clucks.

A donkey brays.

A goose honks.

A chick peeps.

A horse neighs.

A lion roars.

An elephant trumpets.

A wolf howls.

A deer bellows.

An owl hoots.

A bird sings.

A frog croaks.

A rabbit squeaks.

A snake hisses.

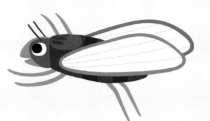

An insect drones.

A bee buzzes.

A bird chirps.

35

The Food Web

The food web is the order in which animals eat to survive.

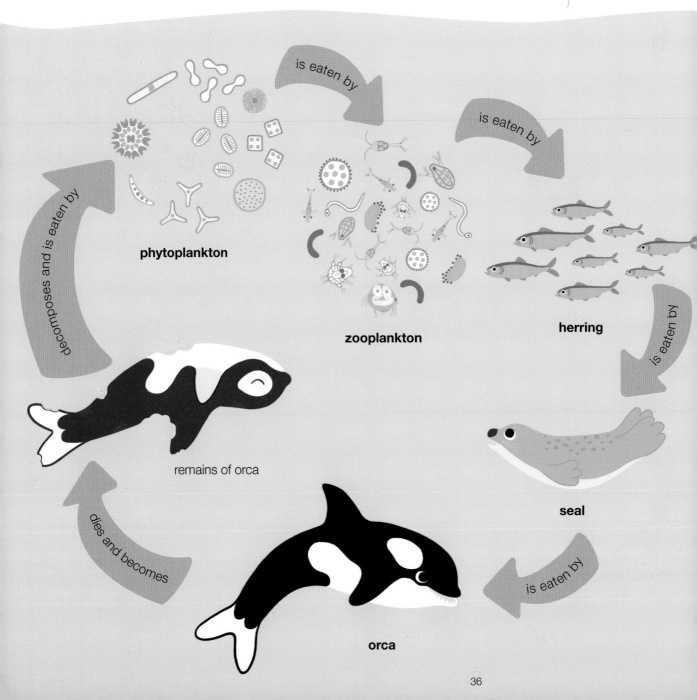

phytoplankton

is eaten by

is eaten by

decomposes and is eaten by

zooplankton

herring

is eaten by

remains of orca

seal

dies and becomes

is eaten by

orca

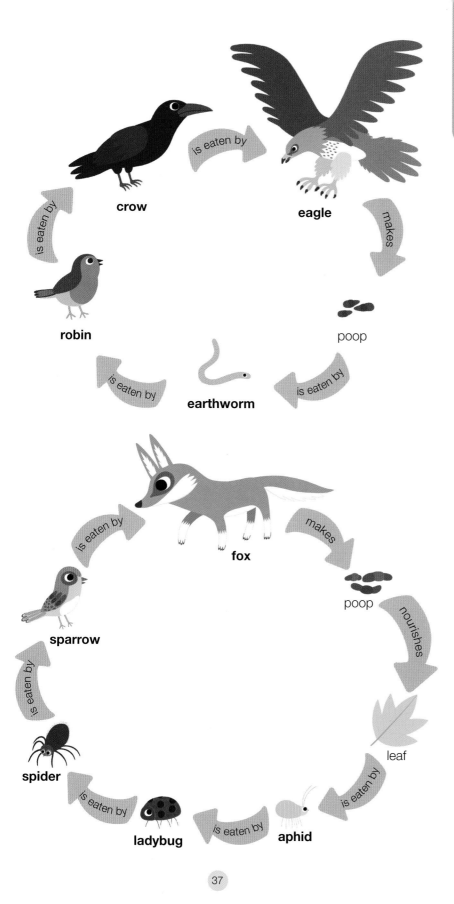

crow

is eaten by

eagle

makes

poop

is eaten by

earthworm

is eaten by

robin

is eaten by

fox

makes

poop

nourishes

leaf

is eaten by

aphid

is eaten by

ladybug

is eaten by

spider

is eaten by

sparrow

is eaten by

Who
are the greatest predators **?**

Animals that hunt other animals are called predators. The ones that get hunted are called prey. At the top of the food web are apex predators.

Lions, tigers, polar bears, and great white sharks are examples of apex predators, which are animals that don't have any natural predators.

However, humans are predators of these animals. Some people hunt these apex predators not for food, but for sport or for parts of their bodies.

Diet **12**
Threatened or Endangered **84**

🏆 Fastest, Tallest, and More!

Animals can be huge or tiny, extremely fast or extremely slow. Here's how some of them measure up.

Anacondas are one of the world's longest snakes!

Standing about 18 feet (5.5 meters) tall, the giraffe is the world's tallest animal.

Sperm whales can dive to around 6,500 feet (2,000 meters) deep and hold their breath for 90 minutes!

The Galápagos tortoise usually lives more than 100 years.

Ants can lift 20 times their own body weight. If you were as strong as an ant, you would be able to lift a car!

The blue whale is the heaviest animal in the world, weighing around 330,000 pounds (150,000 kilograms).

African elephants are the largest of all land animals. They can weigh up to 14,000 pounds (6,350 kilograms).

When diving to catch their prey, peregrine falcons are the fastest, flying up to 200 miles (320 kilometers) per hour.

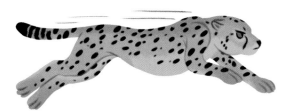

Cheetahs are the fastest land animal. They can run at a speed of more than 60 miles (97 kilometers) per hour.

How
have animals helped people ?

Animals can be heroes! At sea, dolphins will sometimes help sailors by alerting them to danger.

Some breeds of dogs are trained for search and rescue operations. These include German shepherds and Labrador retrievers.

Well known for their keen sense of smell, these dogs can also find people trapped in avalanches.

Types of Animals 14
Home 74

Let's Review!

Match each animal with its home.

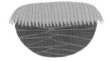

Do you know why this peacock is displaying his feathers?

Why might this tortoise be hiding in its shell?

Who eats whom? Point to these animals in the order they would eat each other in the food web.

crow

robin

eagle

earthworm

You can tell a cat is scared when it arches its
back or tucks in its tail. A dog wags its tail when it is happy.
A chimpanzee puckers its lips because it wants to cuddle.
How do you express your feelings?

Animal
Habitats

African Savanna

A savanna is usually flat, dry grassland, with few trees and shrubs. Animals hunt for food to survive, while watching out for predators.

hyenas

zebras

wildebeests

lions watching their prey

gazelles

crossing the river

leopard

cattle egret

flamingos

crocodile

hippopotamus

buffalo

rhinoceroses

hunting

cheetah

baboon

giraffe

drinking

lion cubs playing

African elephants

bathing

Where
is the savanna
?

There are savannas on many continents, but the largest are in Africa. Savannas can also be found in Australia, North and South America, and Asia.

People in the savanna experience two seasons, dry and wet. During the wet, or rainy, season, it is extremely hot and humid.

The savanna is home to many animals. It is possible to see them in their natural habitat by going on a safari.

Rain Forests

Rain forests around the world are home to millions of species of mammals, birds, reptiles, and insects.

leopard

African forest buffalo

caiman

tiger

Asian elephants

okapis

pangolin

capybara

anteater

chameleon

mosquito

toucan

sloth

armadillo

parrot

snake

macaque

orangutans

gorilla

Where
can you find rain forests ?

Have you and your friends pretended to be animals in the rain forest?

Tropical rain forests are found in regions near the equator, where there is a lot of rain, and it is hot all year round.

Trees in rain forests are really tall, and its dense layers make them great places to hide.

Types of Animals **14**
Rain Forest at the Zoo **62**

Mountains

Here, animals can be found grazing in the pastures, climbing on rocks, or safe at home in their caves.

snow

bald eagle

vole

grouse

bearded vulture

eaglets

nest

griffon vulture

fir

marmot

hiking

fishing

stream

trout

bear

salmon

trail

goat

tending sheep

waterfall

rocks

ibex

mouflon

lynx

mountain hare

sheep

wolves

Where
do some animals go in the winter **?**

If you've been to the mountains in the winter, you might have wondered where all the animals are. Where could they be hiding?

Animals stay safe and warm in the winter. The mountain hare's home is a well-hidden burrow. It comes out at night to feed on plants and grasses.

In the winter, voles stay active, but they huddle together in their underground nests. Marmots, on the other hand, sleep all winter long in their burrows.

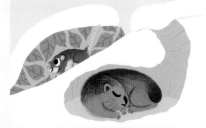

Shelter **28**
Sleep **30**

By the Sea

Look in the sand, on or under rocks, or in the water. There are lots of animals to be found around the seashore.

sea star

crab

sargo

hermit crab

whelk

razor clam

lionfish

weever hiding in the sand

grouper

cockleshell

sea urchin

mackerel

squid

limpet

cuttlefish

seahorse

moray eel

octopus

jellyfish

lobster

rabbit

sand dune

sand flea

sea anemone

winkle

shrimp

blenny

gull

How
do you find tiny creatures ?

At the beach, you don't always see the little animals around you. You may have to do a bit of digging to find them.

You can uncover shellfish by raking the sand. Be sure to use a tool when picking up a sea urchin. Its spines are pointy and may sting!

Look for crabs under small rocks, and lots of shrimp in tide pools.

Night Forest

Many creatures are active at night. You may come across these animals in your backyard, or in the forest.

barred owl

cat

eagle owl

deer

toad

glowworm

bugs

bat

badger

moth

hare

tawny owl

fox

vole

bear

deer

cuckoo

gudgeons

weasel

beaver

raccoon

wild boars

What are nocturnal animals ?

Nocturnal animals are creatures that hunt, feed, and play at night. Lots of animals take the opportunity to come out after the sun goes down.

During the day, people are outside; there can be a lot of activity and noise. At night, it is quieter. The darkness also protects animals from their enemies.

In the African savanna, it is also much cooler at night, which is why the animals there prefer to come out then.

Types of Animals **14**

Sleep **30**

Backyard

When the weather is nice, you will find lots of animals out and about in the backyard.

swallow

snake

mouse

magpie

robin

nest

squirrel

birdhouse

chickadee

butterfly

sparrow

dragonfly

slug

woodpecker

mole

shrew

salamander

hedgehog

caterpillar

snail

crow

frog

tadpoles

You will also notice little creatures such as insects, spiders, and worms.

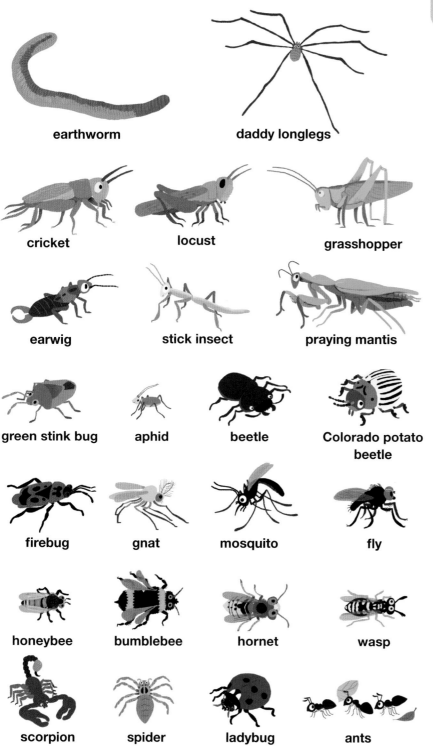

earthworm

daddy longlegs

cricket

locust

grasshopper

earwig

stick insect

praying mantis

green stink bug

aphid

beetle

Colorado potato beetle

firebug

gnat

mosquito

fly

honeybee

bumblebee

hornet

wasp

scorpion

spider

ladybug

ants

How
do insects help us ?

You may think of insects as pests. Some of them, such as mosquitoes, bite. Locusts can destroy crops, and flies can spread disease.

However, insects can be very helpful creatures! The ladybug, for instance, eats aphids, which feed on plants.

Butterflies are also important. They help carry pollen, which plants need to make seeds. Bees feed on the nectar of flowers to create delicious honey.

Let's Review!

Match each of these animals with its habitat.

snail

macaque

ibex

seahorse

How are these little critters helpful?

Can you name the creatures? Which ones live in the savanna? Which can be found in the rain forest? Which can you see in a backyard? Are there any that live by the sea?

What are animals that are active at night called?
Have you seen any of them where you live?

Observing Animals

Safari Park

A safari park is where you'll see animals from the African savanna.

entrance

wildebeests

giraffe

zebras

African forest buffalo

hay

food trough

gazelles

rhinoceros

warthog

60

flamingo

hippopotamuses

baboon

African elephant

water trough

lions

ostrich

security fence

How
do zoos care for animals ?

In many cities around the world, zoos are built to introduce wild animals to the public.

The zoos have veterinarians and health experts who care for the animals. They also take part in wildlife conservation and education efforts.

The animals are fed and checked daily, and their enclosures are kept clean. The zookeepers plan activities that encourage natural behavior from the animals.

African Savanna **44**
Deserts: Hot and Cold **64**

🌴 Rain Forest at the Zoo

Here, you'll discover animals from rain forests, humid places with tall trees and dense foliage.

pangolin

cleaning the cage

African forest buffalo

okapi

zookeeper

hay

sloth

anteaters

Asian elephant

capybara

leopard

tiger

meat

caiman

macaques

orangutan

tire

fruit

gorilla

Where
do zoo animals come from?

At the zoo, animals live in enclosed spaces and have food brought to them. They get to know the humans who take care of them.

Zoos breed their animals or get them from other zoos. Many are not allowed to capture wild animals to show in a zoo environment.

Most zoo animals would not be able to survive in the wild. They have adapted to life in a zoo and would not know how to hunt for food or defend themselves.

Mammals **16**
Rain Forests **46**

Deserts: Hot and Cold

The zoo is also home to animals that originally come from desert areas, both hot and cold.

koalas

kangaroos

ANIMALS FROM HOT DESERTS

oryx

camels

fennec fox

jackal

meerkats

scooping hay

moose

ANIMALS FROM COLD, OR POLAR, DESERTS

caribou

snowy owl

wandering albatross

bison

arctic fox

Why
won't you see all animals in zoos ?

At the zoo, you can see lots of different species of animals. However, you can't see all of them, because there are too many!

No one knows for sure how many millions of species there are on Earth. Only about 2 million of them have been identified.

It is easier to spot the big animals, but there are millions of tiny creatures that can only be seen through a microscope.

Reptiles and Amphibians

These creatures can be found on every continent except Antarctica.

salamander

Komodo dragon

chameleon

iguana

poison dart frogs

toad

gecko

anaconda

rattlesnake

cobra

grass snake

snakes

frogs

🕷 Little Critters

Hundreds of thousands of species of insects, spiders, and other little critters have been identified, but millions more still haven't been discovered.

| tarantula | scorpion | centipede |

fire ants

rhinoceros beetle

cockroach

black widow spider

butterflies

moths

Molting is part of an animal's growth. It is when creatures shed their skin, either all at once with new skin or a little at a time.

Snakes molt throughout their lives. Bears also molt by shedding their fur. Birds molt at least once a year, replacing their old feathers with new ones.

Humans also molt, but not all at once. We shed hair and skin cells regularly. Scientists note that we shed our entire outer layer of skin every two to four weeks!

 # Aviary

An aviary is a large enclosed space where birds can fly freely. It also includes plants that are native to the birds' natural habitats.

heron

stork

marabou

ibis

flamingos

pelican

Wetlands

macaws

toucan

Tropical Rain Forest

Ostriches

condor

vulture

Large Birds

peacock

How
do birds fly ?

Birds have wings that they can spread out and move up and down. By doing this, the birds create air movement that helps them fly.

Some birds don't need to flap their wings much once they're flying. They use air currents to soar.

From hot-air balloons to biplanes and airliners, humans have invented many ways to take to the skies. Do you have a favorite way to fly?

Types of Animals **14**
Backyard **54**

Aquarium

An aquarium is a zoo for marine animals. You can see all kinds of aquatic creatures from around the world here.

hammerhead shark

guide

ray

small-spotted catshark

sharks and rays

mangrove

piranha

four-eye butterfly fish

turtles

mangrove plants and creatures

animal health center

feeding

treating

breeding tanks

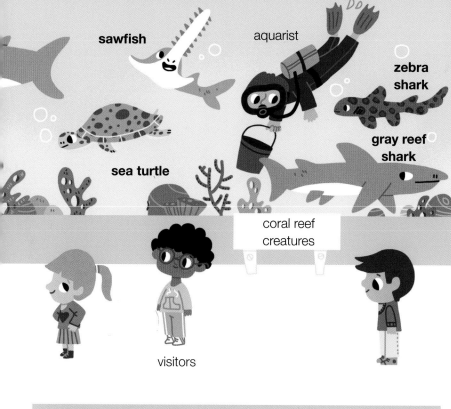

sawfish

aquarist

zebra shark

gray reef shark

sea turtle

coral reef creatures

visitors

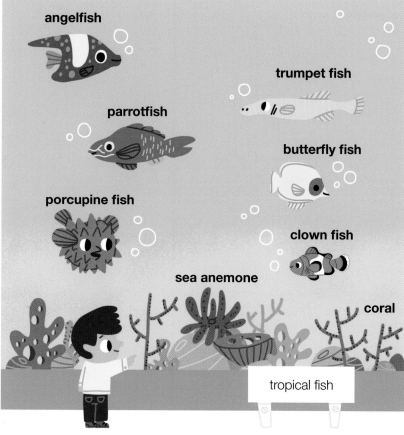

angelfish

trumpet fish

parrotfish

butterfly fish

porcupine fish

clown fish

sea anemone

coral

tropical fish

How
do fish breathe underwater

?

On the sides of a fish's head are several long slits. These are its gills, which fish use to help them breathe.

Fish get oxygen from the water. Water goes into a fish's mouth, then passes over the gills, which absorb the oxygen in the water.

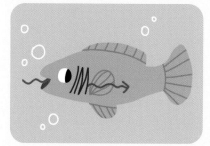

Not all sea creatures can breathe underwater. Mammals, including dolphins and whales, have to come up to the surface of the water to breathe—just like you!

Types of Animals **14**
By the Sea **50**

Pet Store

At a pet store, you can find many animals to take care of in your home.

parrot

canary

pet toys

parakeet crested parakeets

dry dog food

wet cat food

birdseed

food bowls

collars

leashes

cage

turtles

goldfish

saltwater fish

chinchillas

mice

dwarf rabbits

hamsters

dogs

You may have seen squirrels or birds in your backyard and wanted to keep them as pets.

However, these creatures are not tame. Like lions, wild animals are not meant to live in a house with humans. They need space to roam and hunt.

Some people like to have unusual animals, such as a snake or a spider, as pets. Pet owners have to know how to keep them safe.

aquarium decorations

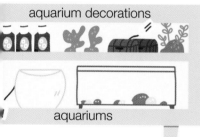

aquariums

cats

gerbil

guinea pigs

 Home

Having a pet is a big responsibility. Whether it's a dog, cat, rabbit, or turtle, there are many things you can do to take care of it.

feeding

going for a walk

training

picking up poop

playing

cleaning the litter box

changing the water of the aquarium

petting

boarding your dog at the kennel

taking your cat on vacation

taking your pet to the vet

bathing

grooming

burying

You teach your pet to pee outdoors or in the litter box, to not jump on strangers, and even to perform tricks.

Just as there are rules for people living in the house, there are rules for animals too. It makes living together more peaceful.

Animals trained to help are called service animals. Guide dogs help blind people get around by looking out for dangers and obstacles that could be in their path.

Pet Store 72
Riding Center 76

Riding Center

Some children learn to ride and take care of horses.

pony

rider

horse trailer

helmet

crop

boots

harness

saddlery

saddles

outdoor arena

clubhouse

instructor

training

riding

76

horse

field

foal, or baby horse

stable

bathing

brushing

saddling

indoor arena

obstacle

sawdust

Flame, Caramel, or Tornado . . . the pony you ride has a name. It recognizes the sound and the tone of your voice when you call it.

Tornado!

Tornado

We give our pets names to connect with them. They become our friends. Names are also useful when you need to fill out information about your pet.

Tornado

There are many names you can give your pet. Some animals are named after favorite characters from TV shows or books. What would you name a pet?

Mimi

Fifi

Pet Store **72**

Home **74**

Educational Farm

Here, children are invited to feed the chickens, milk the cows, and learn about farm life.

rooster

water trough

beehive boxes

chicken coop

hen

young goats, or **kids**

chicks

pasture

donkey

turkey

tractor

toolshed

stable

horse

draft horse

goat

tools

duck and ducklings

78

pigpen

pigs

barn

cow

milking

geese

farmer

calf

visitors

hay

rabbits

farmer

dog

wheelbarrow

trailer

cat

education center

sheep pen

ram

ewe **lamb**

The milk you drink was bought at a store. But do you know how it got there?

Cows produce milk in their udders to feed their calves. On some farms, cows are milked by hand. On other farms, machines may be used.

After the milk is collected, it is pasteurized to keep it fresh, then packaged in plastic jugs or cartons before being delivered to the stores.

Animal Bodies **10**
Mammals **16**

How many animals can you identify by their shadows?

Which of these animals don't make good pets? Why?

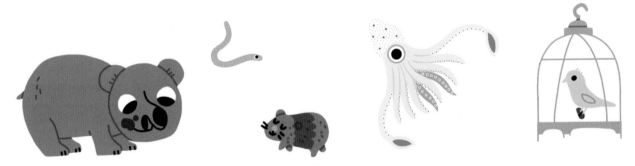

Which of these animals live in hot places? Which live in cold places?

Which insects are these? What differences do you notice between the two groups?

Which of these animals can be found on a farm?

What are some tasks involved in taking care of pets?
If you have a pet, how do you take care of it?

Dinosaurs

These enormous beasts lived on Earth until about 66 million years ago.

Diplodocus

Stegosaurus

Iguanodon

Struthiomimus

Ankylosaurus

Parasaurolophus

Velociraptor

Brachiosaurus

Tyrannosaurus

Triceratops

Baryonyx

⚠ Threatened or Endangered

Many animals on Earth are in danger of becoming extinct, or dying out. One of the reasons why is because people are taking over their habitats.

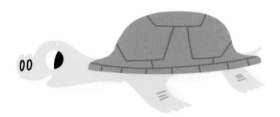

pig-nosed turtle

yellow-crested cockatoo

Irrawaddy dolphin

mountain gorilla

panda

Bengal tiger

humphead wrasse

mossy leaf-tailed gecko

Asian elephant

Atlantic bluefin tuna

some species
of **corals**

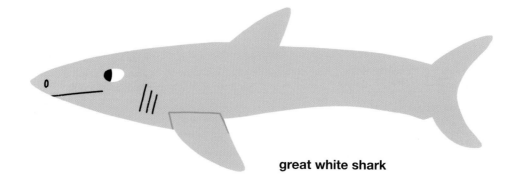

great white shark

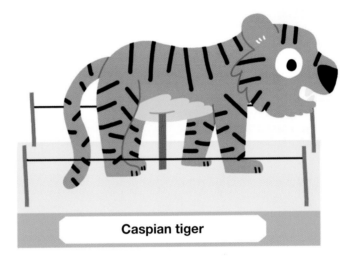Extinct Animals

Some species have already disappeared from Earth because they were overhunted or their habitat changed.

Caspian tiger

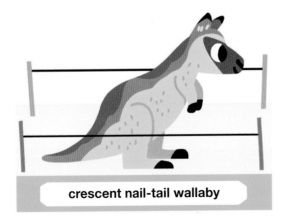

crescent nail-tail wallaby

dodo

Atlas bear

passenger pigeon

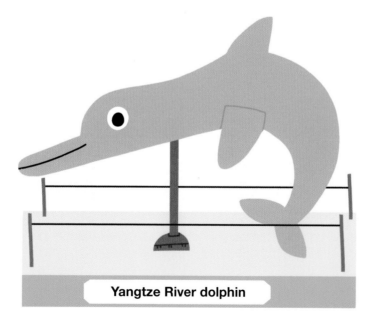

Yangtze River dolphin

🐾 Footprints

Just as you leave footprints in the sand or snow, animals leave their footprints, or tracks, too. The tracks shown here are actual size.

wolf

hedgehog   weasel

cat

bear

dog

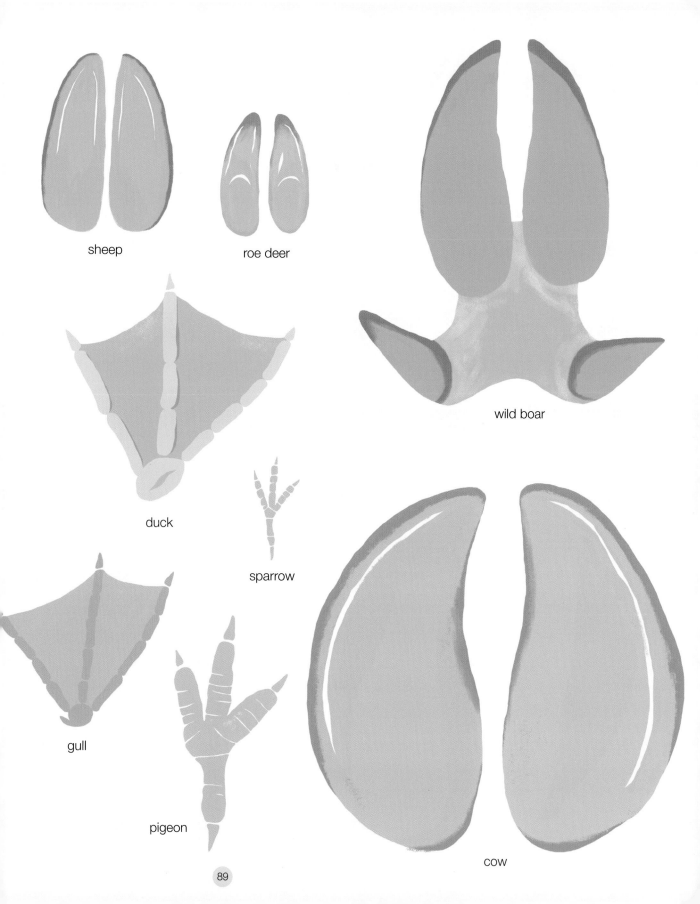

sheep

roe deer

wild boar

duck

sparrow

gull

pigeon

cow

Index

DO YOU KNOW?™ series

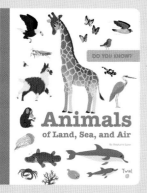

978-2-40803-356-9

978-2-40802-467-3

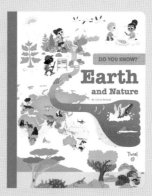

978-2-40803-357-6

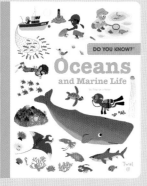

978-2-40802-466-6

978-2-40802-916-6

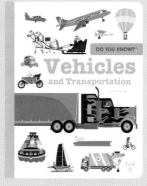

978-2-40802-915-9

ULTIMATE BOOK™ series

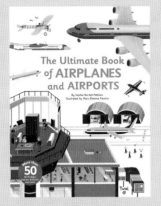

979-1-02760-303-9

979-1-02761-000-6

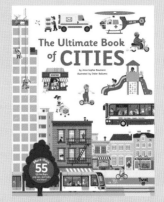

979-1-02760-079-3

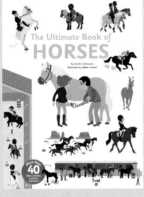

979-1-03631-359-2

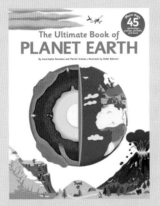

979-1-02760-562-0

979-1-02760-197-4

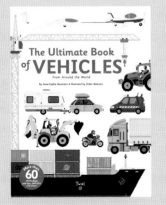

978-2-84801-942-0

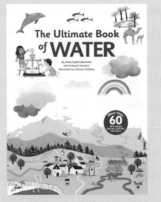

979-1-03633-879-3

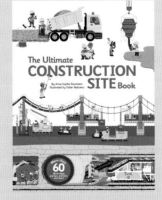

978-2-84801-984-0